True Ju
and
Peace

Concluding Address by
HAZRAT MIRZA MASROOR AHMAD
Khalifatul-Masih V^{aba}
5th successor to the Promised Messiah^{as} and Worldwide
Head of the Ahmadiyya Muslim Community
at the Annual Convention of the Ahmadiyya Muslim
Community UK on August 23, 2015

ISLAM INTERNATIONAL PUBLICATIONS LIMITED

TRUE JUSTICE AND PEACE
Concluding Address by
Hazrat Mirza Masroor Ahmad
Khalifatul-Masih V^{aba}
5th successor to the Promised Messiah^{as} and Worldwide Head of the
Ahmadiyya Muslim Community,
at the Annual Convention of the Ahmadiyya Muslim Community
UK on August 23, 2015

First published in UK in 2016

© Islam International Publications Limited

Published by
Islam International Publications Ltd
(Additional Wakaalat-e-Tasneef, UK)
Islamabad, Sheephatch Lane
Tilford, Surrey
United Kingdom GU10 2AQ

Printed in UK at
Raqeem Press
Farnham, Surrey

ISBN: 978-1-84880-884-3

ABOUT THE AUTHOR

His Holiness, Mirza Masroor Ahmad, Khalifatul-Masih V^{aba}, is the supreme head of the worldwide Ahmadiyya Muslim Community. He is the fifth successor of the Promised Messiah and Reformer, Hazrat Mirza Ghulam Ahmad^{as} of Qadian.

His Holiness was born on September 15, 1950 in Rabwah, Pakistan to the late Mirza Mansoor Ahmad and the late Nasirah Begum Ahmad.

Elected to the lifelong position of Khalifah (Caliph) of the Ahmadiyya Muslim Community on 22nd April 2003, His Holiness serves as the worldwide spiritual and administrative head of an international religious organization with tens of millions of members spread across more than 200 countries.

Since being elected Khalifah, His Holiness has led a worldwide campaign to convey the peaceful message of Islam, through all forms of print and digital media. Under his leadership, national branches of the Ahmadiyya Muslim Community have launched campaigns that reflect the true and peaceful teachings of Islam. Ahmadi Muslims the world over are engaged in grassroots efforts to distribute millions of 'Peace' leaflets to Muslims and non-Muslims alike, host interfaith and peace symposia and present exhibitions of the Holy Qur'an to present its true and noble message. These campaigns have received worldwide media coverage and demonstrate that Islam champions peace, loyalty to one's country of residence and service to humanity.

In 2004, His Holiness launched the annual National Peace Symposium in which guests from all walks of life come together to exchange ideas on the promotion of peace and harmony. Each year, the symposium attracts many serving ministers, parliamentarians, politicians, religious leaders and other dignitaries.

His Holiness has travelled globally to promote and facilitate service to humanity. Under the leadership of His Holiness, the Ahmadiyya Muslim Community has built a number of schools and hospitals that provide excellent education and healthcare facilities in remote parts of the world.

His Holiness strives to establish peace at every level of society. He constantly advises members of the Ahmadiyya Muslim Community to carry out a 'Jihad' (or struggle) of the self to strive to reform individually, which is the true and biggest form of 'Jihad,' so that every Ahmadi Muslim can establish peace on an individual level first of all, and then be enabled to help others also find peace.

His Holiness gives the same message to all others. In response to a question relating to peacebuilding by a non-Muslim guest at a special reception in Melbourne, His Holiness said: "If you have peace in you, it means that you are projecting peace. And if every one of us had peace, it means that we would be projecting peace to others."

At an individual and collective level, on local, national and international platforms, His Holiness is striving to advise all others of the practical means of establishing peace, based on the true teachings of Islam.

His Holiness, Mirza Masroor Ahmad[aba] currently resides in London, England. As spiritual leader of Ahmadi Muslims all over the world, he vigorously champions the cause of Islam through a refreshing message of peace and compassion.

Concluding Address by Hazrat Mirza Masroor Ahmad[aba], 5th successor to the Promised Messiah[as] and Worldwide Head of the Ahmadiyya Muslim Community, at the Annual Convention of the Ahmadiyya Muslim Community UK on August 23, 2015.

❴ Translated from Urdu ❵

After reciting the customary Islamic invocations of *Tashhahhud*[1], *Ta'awwuz*[2] and *Surah al-Faatihah*[3] His Holiness proceeded to recite:

اِنَّ اللّٰهَ يَأْمُرُ بِالْعَدْلِ وَالْاِحْسَانِ وَاِيْتَآئِ ذِي الْقُرْبٰى وَيَنْهٰى عَنِ الْفَحْشَآءِ وَالْمُنْكَرِ وَالْبَغْيِ يَعِظُكُمْ لَعَلَّكُمْ تَذَكَّرُوْنَ

"Verily, Allah enjoins justice, and the doing of good to others; and giving like kindred; and forbids indecency, and manifest evil, and wrongful transgression. He admonished you that you may take heed."[4]

The disorder and corruption widespread in the world today have distressed every peace-loving person. Everyone with sympathy and compassion towards humanity is astonished and worried about the current state of affairs in the world. Much has been said and written about this issue, suggesting that this unrest has arisen much more intensely in the Islamic world or that it is being caused by Muslims. And therefore the conclusion is drawn that religion in general, and Islam in particular (God forbid), is the root of this discord. Up until now, the Western world believed that all of this turmoil would remain limited to the Islamic or underdeveloped nations and that it is exclusively a problem confined to them; and that they (that is, the developed nations) would continue to help them (the underdeveloped nations) in the name of resolving these problems and trying to establish justice.

It is a matter aside that on the pretext of helping and establishing justice, one of their goals was to secure their superiority and to take advantage of the resources of these (underdeveloped) countries. Indeed, certain major powers and anti-religious forces were seriously mistaken. Time has now shown that this is not a problem confined to the Muslim world alone. The tendency towards extremism and terrorism is not limited to the Islamic World; rather, it has in fact spilled over to the West and the developed parts of the world and is about to become a source of great fear and the cause of horrific consequences for them as well.

For the past few years, I have been directing their attention towards the fact that the world is in a state of turmoil. Today, it is an error to believe that this situation is confined to a small part of the world. Whilst the majority would agree with my words and explanations, afterwards they would say that they did not think that the world—especially the developed world—would face the horrific situation that "he" has portrayed. However, today their leaders and those who observe world affairs closely have started to say that even the developed world is not safe from this chaos and the terrifying circumstances that stand before us. Thus, the British Prime Minister's statement also expresses this perilous predicament. The Foreign Minister of Australia has also expressed a similar concern. The former Army Chief of the United Kingdom has voiced similar thoughts. Various newspapers have also started writing on this. The reality is that the world today is enveloped in cruelty and disorder. The developed and well-educated class of people believe that the root cause of this problem is religion, which has now reached its extremes because of a certain Muslim group or organisation. Yet in reality, the root cause of this is their failure to understand religion. The world thinks that we should eschew religion in order to end this disorder and there is abundant propaganda promoting this notion. The press and media also plays its part by saying that religion either makes a person ignorant and dull, or turns him into an extremist. They say that one can only progress by shunning religion and believe that advancement can be achieved by moving away from God Almighty. And due to the spread of this false notion the number of people who deny the existence of God is increasing on a daily basis.

The reality is however, that the world is in disorder because it has forgotten God Almighty. This disorder is either because of the misuse of God Almighty's teachings and using the name of God as a pretext for one's own benefit, or it is due to the denial of God's existence altogether. In fact, they mock God's existence and cross all limits of decency.

In short, the main reasons for the state of disorder in the world are the acquisition of personal gains in the name of God, the true fear of God disappearing from people's hearts, or the denial of the existence of God Almighty whilst giving preference to worldly laws and ideologies. Despite being the creation of Allah the Almighty, man considers Allah the Almighty's customs and system of justice and equity inferior to his man-made customs and system of justice. Man asks: why can we not subordinate religious knowledge and Islamic teachings to our worldly customs, worldly desires and worldly laws according to the needs of the time? A learned university professor has asked this question of me as well. But we should remember that this question could be raised if religious teachings had been corrupted and human values and principles had been proven superior to the foundational values and principles of religion. However, we believe in the book that has been safeguarded for 1400 years and whose teachings are superior in all respects. It is a complete code of life for human beings for all times. It has been revealed by God Almighty, Who is the Lord of the Universe and the Omniscient. Why does it need to be subservient to man-made rules and laws? The purpose of religion is to make people follow it. It does not follow the world or the desires of people. Today, Islam is the religion and the Qur'an is the book which is a guide for all of mankind for all times, under the condition that man has the ability to comprehend it. The rights that are being usurped in the world in this day and age is not the fault of religion. Instead, they are caused by people who deceive others in the name of worldly laws or religion. The injustices that are being carried out in wars in the world today are not caused by religion; rather, they are being carried out by those who only seek materialistic gains. The immorality and shocking scenes of indecency in the name of freedom today are not part of religious teachings; rather, they are due to the degradation caused by man-made laws which have destroyed the commandments of Allah the Almighty. To express one's power, prowess and superiority is not the teaching of Allah the Almighty. Rather, it is an invention of man, because he considers himself superior to everything.

Therefore, whatever we are witnessing in the world today is due to man considering himself to be the wisest and his being devoid of the light of revelation. This exact state of affairs is mentioned in the Holy Qur'an in the following manner:

ظَهَرَ الْفَسَادُ فِي الْبَرِّ وَالْبَحْرِ بِمَا كَسَبَتْ اَيْدِى النَّاسِ لِيُذِيْقَهُمْ بَعْضَ الَّذِىْ عَمِلُوْا لَعَلَّهُمْ يَرْجِعُوْنَ

"Corruption has spread on land and sea because of what man's hands have wrought, that He may make them taste the fruit of some of their doings so that they may turn back from evil."[5]

Due to this mayhem created by man, neither are the rich or poor safe nor are the religious (that is, the so-called religious people) or the irreligious. It is clear that under these circumstances man will be seized and punished by God Almighty. This is a natural consequence of moving away from the Creator. Naturally, when we move away from God Almighty, Who is the Creator and Master, then this should be and in fact is the obvious result: receiving some form of punishment from God Almighty. However, only God Almighty knows and He is a better judge of the punishment which will be given in the hereafter for their actions. But God Almighty is never pleased by punishing His creation. When God Almighty sees His creation treading upon the right path and avoiding disorder, He is happier than a mother who rejoices to find her child after him being lost in dreadful circumstances. A mother searches for her child like an insane person and walks around in both hope and despair, wondering whether the child is alive or not. Then, suddenly she finds and embraces him. However, God Almighty loves His creation even more than this. When a man moves towards Him, God is happier than [that mother]. It is as a result of this love that God Almighty sends His prophets and messengers to reform the world and show them the right path, so that the world is saved from destruction and becomes safe from the punishment due to wrong deeds and disorderliness. God Almighty desires to save His people from falling into the pit of fire, and not only desires to save them from falling into the pit of fire but also to favour them with His rewards.

Regarding these circumstances and this era, the Promised Messiah[as] states that:

"At this moment in time people yearn for spiritual water and yet the earth is completely barren and lifeless. This has become the embodiment of an era whereby

$$\text{ظَهَرَ الْفَسَادُ فِى الْبَرِّ وَالْبَحْرِ}$$

'Corruption has spread on land and sea.'[6] The jungle and sea have become corrupt. The 'jungle' is understood to be the disbelievers and the 'sea' is understood to be the people of the book. It can also mean ignorant people and knowledgeable people. Hence, there is disorder in every section of society. Whichever aspect or facet you look at the world we see it is transformed. Spirituality no longer exists and nor is its impact visible any longer. Whether young or old, all are engulfed in immorality. It appears that the worship of God and the knowledge of His being have been completely extinguished. Right now it is necessary for heavenly water and the [spiritual] radiance of prophethood to descend and enlighten those hearts which are willing. Express gratitude to God Almighty! For He has sent His spiritual light in this day and age through His Grace. There are few, how-

ever, who derive benefit from this spiritual light."[7]

Thus, in order to save humanity, God the Exalted acts according to His Sunnah [way]. He continues to send His messengers in order to guide mankind and to show them ways of safeguarding themselves from disorders. In this era He has sent the Promised Messiah[as] [Hazrat Mirza Ghulam Ahmad[as] of Qadian]. The current state of the world shows that the state of the Muslims has deteriorated – one of the speakers also mentioned this with reference to a certain country – and so too have [deteriorated] the followers of other faiths and also those who do not follow any religion. The world is running towards what it thinks is water. However, it is not water—it is a mirage. The true water and spiritual light is that which has been sent down by God Almighty. The Muslim world and the rest of the world should be thankful and should be guided by this spiritual light and drink from this oasis. Instead, they are immersed in darkness and drinking from dirty ponds. Unfortunately, the Muslims are not showing any regard for the true servant of the Holy Prophet[sa], [the Promised Messiah[as]]. Thinking the dirty water to be clean, they follow the teachings of malicious scholars. Others are also making excuses instead of recognising the true faith; consequently, the world today is completely abandoning faith. They are totally denying the existence of God Almighty. Though the majority of Muslims are firm in their faith to the extent of claiming [themselves to be Muslims] or in their dogma; however, the 'Ulema [scholars] have profoundly spoilt their education and practice by blinding their intellect. This is not an accusation which I am levelling against them; rather this is the truth which is visible to all. The disorder in the Muslim world, including the bloodshed and other extremist acts in the name of religion, God or the Prophet, are apparent to all. The injustices of the governments on their people and also the rebellious attitude of the people of the country and their injustices is a proof of this. When the general public seeks guidance from its 'Ulema [scholars] they find in them nothing but their own selfish desires. We can see how the words of the Holy Prophet[sa] were fulfilled to the absolute letter when he said that apart from disorder nothing else would be found emanating from these scholars. There would be contradiction in their speech and action and apart from ignorance and discord, nothing else will be gained from them.[8]

Thus, the statements and behaviour of today's 'Ulema [scholars] are in fact proof of the Holy Prophet's[sa] truthfulness. Further, Muslims have generally fallen victim to moral degeneration and the decline in their faith is also quite evident. The state of the general Muslims would be quite obvious when the 'Ulema [scholars] are themselves so ignorant and pass edicts based on their self-interest. For their own interests, these 'Ulema have distorted the teachings of Islam to such an extent that it has even become permissible according to them to usurp the rights of others. Such kinds of edicts are very common in Pakistan now, because Ahmadis are considered to be outside the pale of Islam. Despite the fact that they read and can continue reading

لَآ اِلٰهَ اِلَّا اللّٰهُ مُحَمَّدٌ رَّسُوۡلُ اللّٰهِ

[there is none worthy of worship except Allah; Muhammad[sa] is the messenger of Allah] and since they are not a part of Islam, it is hence permissible to loot and seize their property. Yet, they themselves are split into different sects and the fires of hatred are smouldering. Allah the Exalted states that they are رُحَمَآءُ بَیۡنَہُمۡ "tender among themselves."[9] However, let alone displaying love and brotherhood, deep hatred for one another is thriving among them. Thus, this is evidence that a state of corruption exists amongst the Muslims too. And at such a time, it was a requisite of the mercy of Allah the Exalted, that He should send His messenger.

And indeed, in keeping with His tradition and promise, Hazrat Mirza Ghulam Ahmad of Qadian was sent by Allah the Exalted. However, as I mentioned earlier, that instead of accepting him, the 'Ulema [scholars] mislead the Muslims and have also increased [the Muslims] in their opposition to him. Rather than answering and hearkening to the call of the one who came and fulfilled the instruction of Allah the Exalted and His Prophet, and trying to become a unified *Ummah*, they have become embroiled in disorder, discord and bloodshed among themselves and are also having a negative impact on the rest of the world. That is why the opposing non-Muslim powers are able to take advantage of the weakened state of the Muslims. They are levelling allegations against Islam and attacking it. They are labelling Islam as a religion of chaos, disorder and extremism. They seek to prove that world peace and harmony can only be established by non-Muslims and those who have moved away from religion. However, these powers do not voice this openly, but are carrying out their schemes and ploys in a rather shrewd manner. On the one hand they claim to show sympathy and seek to forge peaceful relations with Muslims by offering their services to eradicate the chaos and disorder from the Muslim world. And on the other hand they state that neither the religion of Islam nor Muslims are bad; Islam does not teach terrorism and transgression and that we should all seek to work together to end the world's disorder, which appears to be more prevalent in the Muslim world. However, on the other side, they also suggest there is a connection between Islam, terrorism and violence. They also say that the extremism is due to the teachings of Islam. They want to appease the powers who oppose Islam as well as the Muslims by telling one leader to say one thing while at the same time telling the others to say the complete opposite.

We say to such people that as far as the teachings of Islam are concerned, they form the basis of peace, security and reconciliation which is unmatched by any other teaching. Those who speak against Muslims should remember that by saying this they are adding further fuel to these so-called Islamic extremist groups. By making such statements, they are playing a role in inciting [those] Muslims who are less educated and frustrated because of their circumstances. Peace cannot be established by blaming religion; rather, it can only be achieved by campaigning against transgression and injustice while keeping religion aside. Success is only attainable if they play their role by campaigning against wrongdoing and oppression. Therefore, those who belong to the superpowers as well as the government leaders need to establish their strategies and policies on justice. There is no doubt that a worldly person does not possess spiritual sight and therefore only sees things from a worldly perspective; the apparent efforts being made for establishing peace are in fact becoming a cause for the disorder. Therefore the superpowers should not take pride in their power. If we seek to establish peace then the worldly powers will have to change their attitude or otherwise the world will become enveloped in violence and wars, with even greater severity. Similarly, Muslims must also listen to the voice of God the Exalted, and need to examine the so-called slogans raised by their pseudo-scholars, and the leaders and organisations in light of those standards contained in God Almighty's teaching. They should see how beautiful the teaching of Islam is! They should try to understand what God expects from them. Allah the Exalted wants them to look to the one who He has sent. When this happens mutual differences will come to an end and love, friendship and justice will be established instead. Muslims will become a united *Ummah* and as a result they will attain freedom and deliverance from the clutches of enslavement from non-Muslim powers.

We should always remember that the Western or

secular education and system are not the guarantors for creating peace and security in the world and nor can they ever be so. The guarantor for creating world peace and security are the teachings of Islam which were neither presented by any religion before Islam nor are they found in any other philosophy, -ism or system in this day and age. Indeed it is the beautiful teachings of Islam which guarantee creating peace and security in the world.

Therefore today, instead of the non-Muslim powers showing us the way to peace and security, we need to show them the true path of peace and justice in light of the Islamic teachings. This teaching manifests its splendour in the short verse that I have just recited. Hence, as opposed to adopting a defensive stance, each and every Muslim should consider putting this remarkable teaching before the world as a challenge. Therefore, today I will also state some things in light of this teaching which was revealed to the Holy Prophet[sa] 1400 years ago. The Holy Prophet[sa] along with his Rightly Guided Khulafaa [Caliphs] and some of the selfless leaders of the state, who felt the pain of the *Ummah*, adhered to this teaching and practised it and thereby established a beautiful society.

I also do not deny the fact that a veil was put over

this beautiful teaching afterwards among the majority of the governments, due to the selfish attitudes and the personal interests of Islamic leaders and scholars. However, as I said, Allah the Exalted sends his prophets and chosen people in every era of disorder and corruption for the guidance of mankind. He also sent the Promised Messiah[as], who clearly expounded upon this beautiful teaching and familiarised us with its beauty. He announced that there was a twofold purpose for my advent: firstly, to unite man with Allah the Exalted and to draw the attention [of man] towards fulfilling the rights of God; secondly, the purpose of his advent was to make one fulfil the rights of fellow human beings.[10]

Hence, Islam draws our attention towards fulfilling these two rights and we must examine this in the light of the teaching of the Holy Qur'an. As I said, in light of this verse of the Holy Qur'an, we can observe how the highest standards of [fulfilling] these rights can be established in the world and the establishment of equality, justice, love and brotherhood. We also observe how well the Holy Prophet[sa] demonstrated this to us through his own practical example. Even in this era, we see how, through this verse, the person who was sent by Allah the Exalted guided us regarding how one should fulfil both these types of rights.

The Promised Messiah[as] states that:

There are two overarching commandments of the Holy Qur'an: firstly, unity, love and obedience of the Creator, glory be to His name; secondly, compassion for one's brothers and fellow human beings. Furthermore, He has split these commands into three stages. With reference to the verse of the Holy Qur'an,

اِنَّ اللّٰهَ يَأْمُرُ بِالْعَدْلِ وَالْاِحْسَانِ وَاِيۡتَآئِ ذِی الْقُرۡبٰی

"Verily, Allah enjoins justice, and the doing of good to others; and giving like kindred."[11] the Promised Messiah[as] comments that in the first instance, the meaning of this verse is that one should display justice in the relationship of obedience with his Creator and should abstain from becoming unjust. Hence, just as in reality, besides Him no one is worthy of worship, no one is worthy of love and no one is worthy of trust because every single right belongs to Him, due to His exclusivity of being the Creator, the Sustainer and the Lord. (It is He who created us, He grants us life and sustenance and He it is Who provides us the means of growth. Hence, this is His right alone.) Similarly, you too should not associate anyone with Him in His worship, in His love and in His Lordship. If you manage to do as much, then this is *'Adl* (justice), and the demonstration of which is obligatory upon you. If you wish to progress further then there is the stage of *Ihsaan* (doing good to others). That [stage] is for you to become so convinced of His Greatness, to become so disciplined in your worship before Him and to become so absorbed in His love, as if you have seen His Majesty, Glory and His infinite Beauty. After this is the stage of *Iitaa-e-Dhil Qurbaa* (giving like kindred). And that [stage] is, for your worship, your love and your obedience to become completely free from pretence and superficiality and for you to remember Him with such intimate friendship as you remember your fathers. Your love for Him should become like the love a child holds for his beloved mother. In the second instance, in terms of compassion for mankind, the meaning of this verse is for you to treat your brothers and fellow humans with justice and not to exceed in taking from them what is due to you (do try to take your rights but do not try to take more than you are due) and establish yourself upon justice. If you wish to progress further from this stage, then the next stage is *Ihsaan* (doing good to others). And this [stage] is when you do good in exchange of a wrong committed by your brother and for you to grant him comfort in exchange for his abuse and to help him, out of compassion and love.

After this, is the stage of *Iitaa-e-Dhil Qurbaa* (giving

like kindred) and that is, that whatever good deed you do for your brother, or whatever good you do for mankind should not be considered as a favour in any way. Rather, it should be done simply owing to one's natural urge and without any ulterior motive (whatever deed you carry out should be done without thinking that you are doing a favour to someone. It should be done without such a thought). It should be done in a manner that is similar to when a relative acts good towards another relative on account of his close relation. This is the ultimate stage of moral development, whereby one shows sympathy to the creation but without any personal interest, or motive. In fact, the passion one has for his brother or close one develops to such a high degree that he naturally does the deed, without any reason, or any kind of gratitude, prayer or its end result.[12]

Thus unless one develops an understanding of fulfilling both these rights, the claims of establishing justice and equality will simply remain as mere claims. Man-made laws do not exceed beyond *'Adl* [justice] and the world thinks that by establishing *'Adl* [justice] they have overcome all stages for the establishment of peace and have thus acquired all that which they set out to acquire; however injustices still exist here as well. The requisites of *'Adl* [justice] cannot be fulfilled when there are personal interests involved. This is true among the rich as well as the poor [parts of the] world. The most they can do is to try and do *Ihsaan* [doing of good to others] but not because the *Ihsaan* is part of their duty, which is why afterwards they remind the person about their favours upon them. We also generally observe in the world, that out of compassion when one even thinks of offering someone more than their right, they stipulate various conditions. Nowadays this is commonly observed in the dealings and practices of the major governments. There are various conditions attached when help is offered to poorer countries. However, Islam teaches that such help after which approbation is sought or one is given injury, is not a virtuous deed. Thus, it states:

$$لَا تُبْطِلُوۡا صَدَقٰتِكُمۡ بِالۡمَنِّ وَالۡاَذٰى$$

"...render not vain your alms by reproach and injury..."[13]

Explaining this, the Promised Messiah[as] states that:

"O ye who extend favours to others! Do not ruin your alms which ought to be on the basis of sincerity, by reproach and injury."[14]

Thus, if the heart is devoid of sincerity and devotion then such alms and aid no longer become a charitable act. The world cannot even entertain the thought of اِيْتَآئِ ذِى الْقُرْبٰى "giving like kindred."[15] As I mentioned earlier, man-made laws cannot go beyond *'Adl* [justice] and even then they are just limited to speech because they are ruined by all kinds of conditions which are attached to them. However, God Almighty enjoins you to do justice, and the doing of good to others and giving like kindred; and to fulfil the requisites of justice and equality. Your acts of benevolence should not be followed with any kind of suffering or pain. Also, you should not just consider *'Adl* and *Ihsaan* to be the ultimate stage, rather, "giving like kindred" should also be kept in view, and you should afford sympathy to others without any personal motive. You should feel the pain of others as if it is your own pain; such is the condition that will make you a Mo'min [true believer].

How great are the commandments revealed by God Almighty and the laws designed by Him! Whereby one cannot be a guarantor of true peace unless one becomes selfless in setting the standards of justice, compassion and love. This is the teaching that enables one to reach the pinnacle in fulfilling the rights of others. With regard to compassion for the creation of God Almighty and establishing peace, let alone man-made laws, no religion can present such a teaching and nor has any religion ever presented it in the past. It is only the teaching of Islam that stands above all others in relation to fulfilling the rights of others and establishing peace. If anyone who ascribes himself as Muslim, or any Islamic government or any other group formed in the name of Islam acts contrary to this teaching or carries out extremist acts, then they are acting against the teaching of the Holy Qur'an. Islam has enjoined its followers to adhere to this teaching for all people and in all circumstances. A wrongful act committed in the name of Islam cannot stand as an argument to suggest that Islam permits a license to commit wrong acts. The critics of Islam, who consider themselves to be the standard-bearers of justice and peace, should also be just when presenting their views. Those leaders or politicians of the West, who give statements that they cannot deny there to be some link between the teaching of Islam and extremism, do so owing to their lack of knowledge or simply because they are unjust in their views. They fail to recognise their own actions whereby under the pretence of justice, they in fact completely obliterate it and perpetrate all kinds of injustices. I do not need to give my personal opinion on this because their own writers have unveiled the reality of their justice and establishing peace. An article, 'The West's Libyan Legacy' by John Wight says, "Out of the many examples of Western military campaigns in recent times, none has been more grievous or disastrous than NATO's 2011 intervention in Libya, which only helped turn the country into a failed state." NATO's intervention "ushered in crisis and chaos as Libyan society promptly fragmented and broke down into the tribal, sectarian, and brutal internecine conflict that has turned a once-functioning state and society into a dystopia into which Islamic State (IS) has gained a foothold..." he further writes that "There were no terrorist training camps in Libya prior to NATO's military intervention." The West was not motivated by the desire to help effect democratic change, but to ensure that the extensive and lucrative oil exploration and economic ties were forged.[16]

Thus, this is a glimpse of the injustices carried out in the name of peace and justice. Similarly, many people have written extensively about the war in Iraq being wrong and on various other injustices. However, the teachings of Islam, which they criticise, in fact consider *'Adl* [justice] as the most basic of virtuous deeds. *'Adl* is not a great deed; rather, Islam considers it as the most basic form of a good deed, while they [the West] raise slogans of justice and equality and deem it as a great deed. If they were to adhere to this we may still say that considering they are worldly people, this indeed is a great deed for them, but as I have mentioned before, their standards of *'Adl* [justice] change when it comes to their personal interests. Islam sets forth a beautiful standard for establishing *'Adl*, as it states:

يَٰٓأَيُّهَا ٱلَّذِينَ ءَامَنُوا۟ كُونُوا۟ قَوَّٰمِينَ لِلَّهِ شُهَدَآءَ بِٱلْقِسْطِ ۖ وَلَا يَجْرِمَنَّكُمْ شَنَآنُ قَوْمٍ عَلَىٰٓ أَلَّا تَعْدِلُوا۟ ۚ ٱعْدِلُوا۟ هُوَ أَقْرَبُ لِلتَّقْوَىٰ ۖ وَٱتَّقُوا۟ ٱللَّهَ ۚ إِنَّ ٱللَّهَ خَبِيرٌۢ بِمَا تَعْمَلُونَ

"O ye who believe! Be steadfast in the cause of Allah, bearing witness in equity; and let not a people's enmity incite you to act otherwise than with justice. Be always just, that is nearer to righteousness. And fear Allah. Surely, Allah is Aware of what you do."[17]

This is the beautiful teaching of Islam, that one must not make false justifications even in enmity. *Qawaam* means to carry out a task properly and consistently. Therefore, a Muslim has been commanded to always carry out justice both properly and consistently and to remember to carry out all his works while keeping the commandments of God Almighty in view. A *Mo'min* [true believer] should fulfil the requisites of justice by dwelling deep into the intricacies of God Almighty's commandments. A *Mo'min* [true believer] should always be mindful of God Almighty's commandments and remain in search of them – when this state develops only then can one be deemed a true Muslim. Always remember the commandment of God Almighty regarding justice, by which a people's enmity should not steer you away from justice. God Almighty not only enjoins Muslims to deal with justice and fairness with the enemy, but also instructs us to increase in our virtuous deeds. As the columnist has written, the war in Libya or the deposing of Gaddafi was purely due to economic factors; it was to gain a firm grip on oil revenue. However, the teaching of the Holy Qur'an which they have criticised as promoting extremism, in fact states that one should not look at the wealth of others with envy. I mentioned this in the USA before politicians and one of the politicians, who was an African-American, came to me and said that what you have mentioned, i.e., not to look at another person's wealth with envy and not to derive any unlawful benefit from it, is a very true and accurate statement, which we are in need of here. Thus, if this is their own state, how can these people then criticise Islam? As I quoted earlier, even their own journalists (I mentioned just one earlier) have now begun to write that it is due to their war in Iraq and unjust policies which have led to the emergence of some Muslim extremist groups. What justice was demonstrated in the Second World War when atom bombs were dropped on two cities in Japan massacring innocent civilians? What human sympathy was demonstrated then and what has happened now for this issue to arise once again? Even today they speak about this incident. However, instead of saying that it was wrong and it should not have happened, they show no remorse for their actions. Clifton Truman, who is the grandson of President Truman [former President of the United States] in an interview said regarding the atom bombs that they were a great thing. He said referring to his grandfather, that he ended the war. He said they saved hundreds of thousands of lives on both sides and that is what his grandfather said was his reason for the decision. He also said that he did not feel that the US ever needed to apologise to Japan. Another columnist wrote in the Daily Telegraph on the 9th of August, that it was justifiable to drop atom bombs on Nagasaki and Hiroshima at the expense of human lives. So this is their attitude and their view. This is their justice! Although the war is fought between soldiers, innocent children, the elderly and women are the ones who die! They seek to contrive all kinds of justifications. However, if an

Islamic group is guilty of any wrong actions they immediately attach its blame to the teaching of Islam. The teaching of Islam, in fact, is one that enjoins justice and the doing of good to others; and giving like kindred in all instances. It rejects all forms of injustices and acts of rebellion. The Holy Qur'an enjoins justice and the example of one who adhered to the Holy Qur'an the most, is to be found in the Holy Prophet[sa]. A Jew once came to the Holy Prophet[sa] to settle a dispute and lodged a complaint against a Muslim. After listening to both parties, the Holy Prophet[sa] passed the verdict against the Muslim and in favour of the Jew.[18]

Today, we observe at both a personal level as well as at a governmental one, loans are taken yet all sorts of excuses are presented when it comes to paying it back. However, when we observe the example of the Holy Prophet[sa] which in fact is the true reflection of the teachings of Islam, we find that that not only did he repay the loan before it was due, but he would return more than the actual sum he had borrowed due to his benevolence.

A reference to wars was made earlier, God Almighty states regarding prisoner of wars:

مَا كَانَ لِنَبِيٍّ اَنْ يَّكُوْنَ لَهٗٓ اَسْرٰى حَتّٰى يُثْخِنَ فِى الْاَرْضِ

"It does not behove a Prophet that he should have captives until he engages in a regular fighting in the land."[19]

At a time when it was a common practice to imprison the people of an enemy tribe, it was Islam that spoke out against it. It is asserted that to imprison someone who has not taken up arms against Islam is in fact against justice and fairness. Today, if any government or so-called government conducts this practice in the name of Islam, it is totally contrary to its teachings and is not permissible.

Regarding prisoners of wars, Islam states:

فَإِمَّا مَنًّا بَعْدُ وَ إِمَّا فِدَآءً

"Then afterwards either release them as a favour or by taking ransom."[20]

Furthermore, kind treatment is extended towards prisoners of war. In the days when such wars broke out, every soldier was responsible for his own military equipment and also for his own freedom if he were captured. And so, [in the instance of becoming a captive] either he would himself try or his relatives would make efforts to make arrangements for his release. At times, certain relatives would become hard-hearted and in order to accumulate more wealth they would simply leave their relative in captivity. If the prisoner did not have any close relatives then distant relatives would act in this manner. At times an individual would not have the means to pay the ransom. Thus, the Holy Qur'an states:

$$\text{وَالَّذِيْنَ يَبْتَغُوْنَ الْكِتٰبَ مِمَّا مَلَكَتْ اَيْمَانُكُمْ فَكَاتِبُوْهُمْ اِنْ عَلِمْتُمْ فِيْهِمْ خَيْرًا ۖ وَّاٰتُوْهُمْ مِّنْ مَّالِ اللّٰهِ الَّذِيْٓ اٰتٰىكُمْ}$$

"And such as desire a deed of manumission in writing from among those whom your right hand possesses, write it for them if you know any good in them; and give them out of the wealth of Allah which He has bestowed upon you."[21]

In other words, among the prisoners of wars there will be some whom you can neither release as a favour, nor can they be freed by their own people paying their ransom. However, if they seek their freedom by earning it through their own skills or talents and thus become able to pay their ransom, then they should be freed, providing it is felt that they will be able to earn a livelihood if set free. In fact, [the Holy Qur'an] goes one step further and enjoins doing good to such prisoners by stating that one should also contribute towards their efforts. Muslims should make a contribution from their own wealth and through financial support they should try to liberate them.

Today, those who raise slogans for justice and fairness do not come anywhere near demonstrating such standards. Certain groups who work for human rights claim to do this kind of work but they cannot even achieve the release of those who have been imprisoned because of their faith or political factors, let alone prisoners of war. As I mentioned earlier, the Muslims have forgotten their religious teachings. If they closely reflect upon their teachings, they would never imprison people the way they are doing without justification and thereby bringing the name of Islam into disrepute. Nonetheless, we were discussing the teaching of Islam and in order to restore the rights of one's freedom, Islam goes to such lengths that even if someone from one's enemies takes part in a war and draws the sword against Muslims, and then is imprisoned due to defeat or any other reason, Islam teaches that Muslims should find means to procure his freedom out of a sense of compassion.

I mentioned earlier how the atom bombs that were dropped in Japan, causing the death of many civilians, is still being justified today. If one looks at the images from that time, they show how a person sitting on a set of stairs became a statue after his skin melted and hung almost instantly. Though there were deaths instantaneously, fatalities continued to occur for a long time afterwards due to the effects of radiation and children were born with disabilities. Now, after so many years, why are they bringing up the subject of the war in Japan and atom bombs? Do they want to incite those who commit injustices?

The Holy Prophet[sa] stated that if one overpowered the enemy during war, even then they were not permitted to disfigure their faces. The enemy was not to be deceived in a state of war, nor was any kind of deception allowed in war.[22]

No children or women were to be killed and nor were any priests or religious leaders. The elderly, children and women were not to be attacked.[23]

Peace and compassion would always be kept in view. If because of the enemy's oppression, one had to go to the enemy's country for war, then they should not cause fear and terror among the general public nor treat them harshly.[24]

The movement of the army should not cause any hindrance or disturbance to the general population either.[25]

The enemy should not be subjected to any disfigurement of the face and the least possible harm should be caused to them.[26]

If a Muslim is guilty of being unlawfully harsh to any prisoner of war then he must immediately free him.[27] Consideration was to be given to the care and comfort of the prisoners; if any of the prisoners were related to one another then they should be kept together and not kept separated.[28]

Whoever had any prisoners must feed them with the same food he ate himself.[29] How can all of this be described? All of this exceeded beyond justice and in fact was *Ihsaan* [doing of good to others]. Who extends such treatment to prisoners?

Never have any previous teachings been able to match this teaching and nor do today's laws of human rights compare to this high standard of *'Adl* and *Ihsaan*. All of the points that I have mentioned regarding prisoners is with the aim of not prolonging wars, but rather stopping them.

When the Holy Prophet[sa] formed the Covenant of Madinah, he afforded the Jews the same rights that Muslims enjoyed. They would not be treated unjustly by any Mo'min [true believer] and if any injustice was carried out against them by any Mo'min or by anyone else, they would be granted help in countering it.[30]

Among many of the conditions [of the covenant], this particular condition was the guarantor of peace for the Jews – whether they stayed in the city of Madinah or went outside of it. This is the justice which was established by the Holy Prophet^{sa}. If Muslims seek to attain this standard [of justice] and fulfil their covenants, then they would never have to face humiliation. The history of the Muslims shows that as long as they fulfilled their covenants they continued to succeed. However, the moment they stopped fulfilling their covenants and relinquished justice, they were humiliated. A great example of fulfilling one's covenant was when the Muslim army had to retreat due to the Roman army's attack. The Muslims returned the tax taken from the non-Muslims of that area and said that they took this tax in order to protect them and establish peace in the area. However, because they could no longer do that, therefore they were not its rightful owners anymore. The response and the reaction of the people from that area is equally a golden chapter in human history, and one that should be written in lustrous terms. They responded that they had become the target of oppression from the people of their own religion; however, Muslims went there and took over and amazed them by fulfilling their covenants and establishing such high standards of justice. They said that now, we shall fight along with you. So, the Muslims were able to fend off the Roman army and the [Muslim] government was re-established. When the Muslims re-entered the city, they were given an exuberant reception by its people.[31]

If only Muslim governments could take a lesson from this. If they stop the injustices upon their own people and on others, they will become the leaders of the world, instead of being humiliated and disgraced. However, for this to happen they must hearken to the call from the Imam of the age. The Holy Qur'an contains countless injunctions regarding the subject of justice, and the doing of good to others and giving like kindred. The life of the Holy Prophet[sa] is also full of such examples. In this age, there are many references of these in the writings of the Promised Messiah[as] too, elaborating on this specific verse:

$$اِنَّ اللّٰهَ يَأْمُرُ بِالْعَدْلِ وَالْاِحْسَانِ وَاِيْتَآئِ ذِی الْقُرْبٰی$$

"Verily, Allah enjoins justice, and the doing of good to others; and giving like kindred..." – if one were to read them all, it could take hours.[32]

Here, I would also like to present another expression of the Holy Prophet's[sa] desire of 'giving like kindred' to men who have strayed away (from God Almighty). It is not only the Mo'mineen [true believers], in fact it is the whole of mankind, including idolaters, disbelievers and people of other faiths (that should be treated like kindred). God Almighty has forever preserved this [expression] in the Holy Qur'an. The Holy Prophet's[sa] sorrow and mercy for those who had strayed away from God Almighty and thereby ruined their hereafter, incurring the displeasure of God Almighty and also His wrath, was even greater than that of one's parents. It kept him anxious all day and would perturb him all night. In other words, the Holy Prophet[sa] endured all kinds of suffering due to his grief for them. Witnessing this anguish and agony, God Almighty stated to him:

$$\text{لَعَلَّكَ بَاخِعٌ نَفْسَكَ اَلَّا يَكُوْنُوْا مُؤْمِنِيْنَ}$$

"Haply thou wilt grieve thyself to death because they believe not."[33]

There can be no greater expression of such heartfelt pain for the whole of mankind than this. The expression of these emotions was not to increase the numbers (of Muslims), rather they were a consequence of his deep concern for mankind. Yet, the critics allege that the actions of groups of Islamic extremists is due to the teachings of Islam, or else they criticise the character of the Holy Prophet[sa] – God forbid. Their actions are a result of them moving away from the true teachings of Islam. Therefore, as I have mentioned before, in order to practise the true teachings of Islam one does not need any extremist Muslim groups, rather the one who has been sent by God Almighty is needed. Also, those who criticise Islam should open their eyes and use their intellects and look at the beautiful teachings of Islam.

Today, it is the duty of every Ahmadi that alongside inculcating the commandment of exacting justice, and the doing of good to others and giving like kindred in all aspects of one's life, they should also convey this message to every individual of the world. They should tell them to listen to the one who has been sent by God Almighty in this age. They should feel the pain he had in the subservience for his beloved master, which God Almighty has described in the same manner: "Haply thou wilt grieve thyself to death because they believe not."[34]

May God Almighty enable us all to develop such sympathy for the whole of mankind! Each person should try to develop this [sympathy] according to the standards and capacity of his own emotions and feelings. Instead of heading towards destruction, may the world save itself by understanding the subject of justice, and the doing of good to others, and giving like kindred! May God Almighty also enable the world to understand this and thereby make the world into a heavenly abode, and also provide the means in this world for the heaven that lies in the hereafter!

We shall now pray. It is a great blessing and favour of God Almighty, that He has truly blessed this convention in every respect, including the attendance and weather also. May God Almighty take you all to your homes safely. Let us pray!"

REFERENCES

1. I bear witness that there is none worthy of worship except Allah; He is One and has no partner; and I bear witness that Muhammad[sa] is His servant and messenger.
2. I seek refuge with Allah, from Satan, the Rejected.
3. First chapter of the Holy Qur'an.
4. The Holy Qur'an, Surah an-Nahl, Verse 91.
5. The Holy Qur'an, Surah ar-Ruum, Verse 42.
6. The Holy Qur'an, Surah ar-Ruum, Verse 42.
7. Hazrat Mirza Ghulam Ahmad[as], Malfuzaat 1985 edition, Vol.4, p.444.
8. See Al-Jaami' Li shu'abil-Imaan Lil-Baihaqi part 3, pp.-317 318, Hadith Number 1763, Maktabah Ar-Rushd 2004.
9. The Holy Qur'an, Surah al-Fath, Verse 30.
10. Hazrat Mirza Ghulam Ahmad[as], See Malfuzaat 1985 edition, Vol. 3, pp.96-95.
11. The Holy Qur'an, Surah an-Nahl, Verse 91.
12. Hazrat Mirza Ghulam Ahmad[as], Izaala-e-Auhaam, Ruhaani Khazaa'in Vol. 3, pp.552-550.
13. The Holy Qur'an, Surah al-Baqarah, Verse 265.
14. Hazrat Mirza Ghulam Ahmad[as], Islaami Usul Ki Filaasafi, Ruhaani Khazaa'in, Vol. 10, p.354.
15. The Holy Qur'an, Surah an-Nahl, Verse 91.
16. John Wight, "'Chaos & Lawlessness': The West's Libyan Legacy," RT.com, published August 2015 ,10, https://www.rt.com/op-edge/-312075libya-chaos-war-west/.
17. The Holy Qur'an, Surah al-Maa'idah, Verse 9.
18. Musnad Ahmad ibn Hanbal, Vol. 5, p.336, Musnad Ibn Abi Hadrad, Hadith number 15570, Aalamul-Kutub, Beirut 1998.

19 The Holy Qur'an, Surah al-Anfaal, Verse 68.
20 The Holy Qur'an, Surah Muhammad, Verse 5.
21 The Holy Qur'an, Surah an-Nuur, Verse 34.
22 Sahih Muslim, Kitaabul-Jihad Was-Siyar, Baabut-Ta'meer Al-Imam Al-Umaraa, Hadith Number 1731.
23 *Musnad Ahmad ibn Hanbal, Vol. 1, p. 768, Musnad 'Abdullah Ibn 'Abbas, Hadith Number 2728, Aalamul-Kutub, Beirut 1998.
24 Sahih Muslim Kitaabul-Jihad Was-Siyar, Baab Fil-amr Bit-Taseer wa tarkit-Takfeer, Hadith Number 1732.
25 Sunun Abi Dawud, Kitaabul-Jihad, Baab Maa Yu'mar Min Inzimaam al-Askar wa Sa'atihi, Hadith Number 2629.
26 Sahih Al-Bukhari Kitaabul-'itaq, Baab Izaa Zuribal-Abdu fal-yajtanib al-wajh, hadith Number 2559.
27 Sahih Muslim, Kitaabul- Aimaan wan-Nuzoor, Baab Suhbat al-mamaaleek wa Kaffaaratu Liman latam 'Abdahu, Hadith Number 1659.
28 Sunan At-Thirmidhi, Abwaabus-Siyar, Baab Fi Kiraahiyatit-Tafreeq Bainas-Sabi, Hadith Number 1566.
29 Sahih Muslim, Kitaabul-Aimaan wan-Nuzoor, Baab It'aamul-mamlook mimmaa ya'akul, Hadith Number 1661
30 As-Sirat-un-Nabawiyyah Li ibn Hisham, pp. 355-354, Hijratur-Rasul[sa], Daarul-Kutub Al-'Ilmiyyah, Beirut 2001.
31 Kitaabul-Khiraaj, Qazi Abu Yusuf, pp 149-151, Faslun Fil Kanaa'is wal-Biya' was-Sulbaan.
32 The Holy Qur'an, Surah An-Nahl, Verse 91.
33 The Holy Qur'an, Surah Ash-Shu'araa', Verse 4.
34 The Holy Qur'an, Surah Ash-Shu'araa', Verse 4.

---

* Sunan Abi Dawud, Kitaabul-Jihad, Baab Fi Duaa-il-Mushrikeen, Hadith Number 2614.